I May Go to Hell, But I'll be Coloring on the Way Down

A Swear Word Adult Coloring Book

By Swearing N' Coloring

ISBN-13: 978-1523666423
ISBN-10: 1523666420

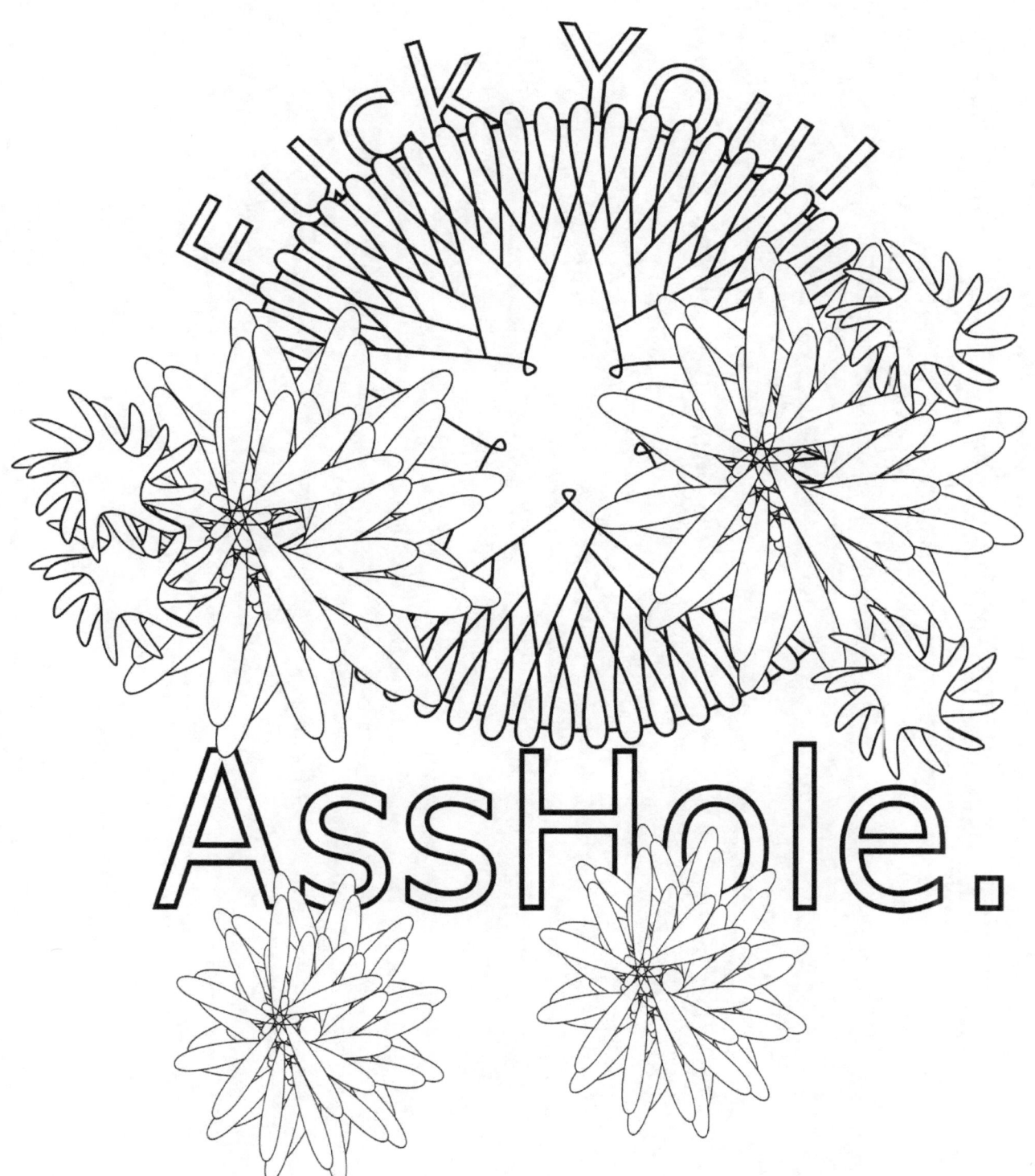

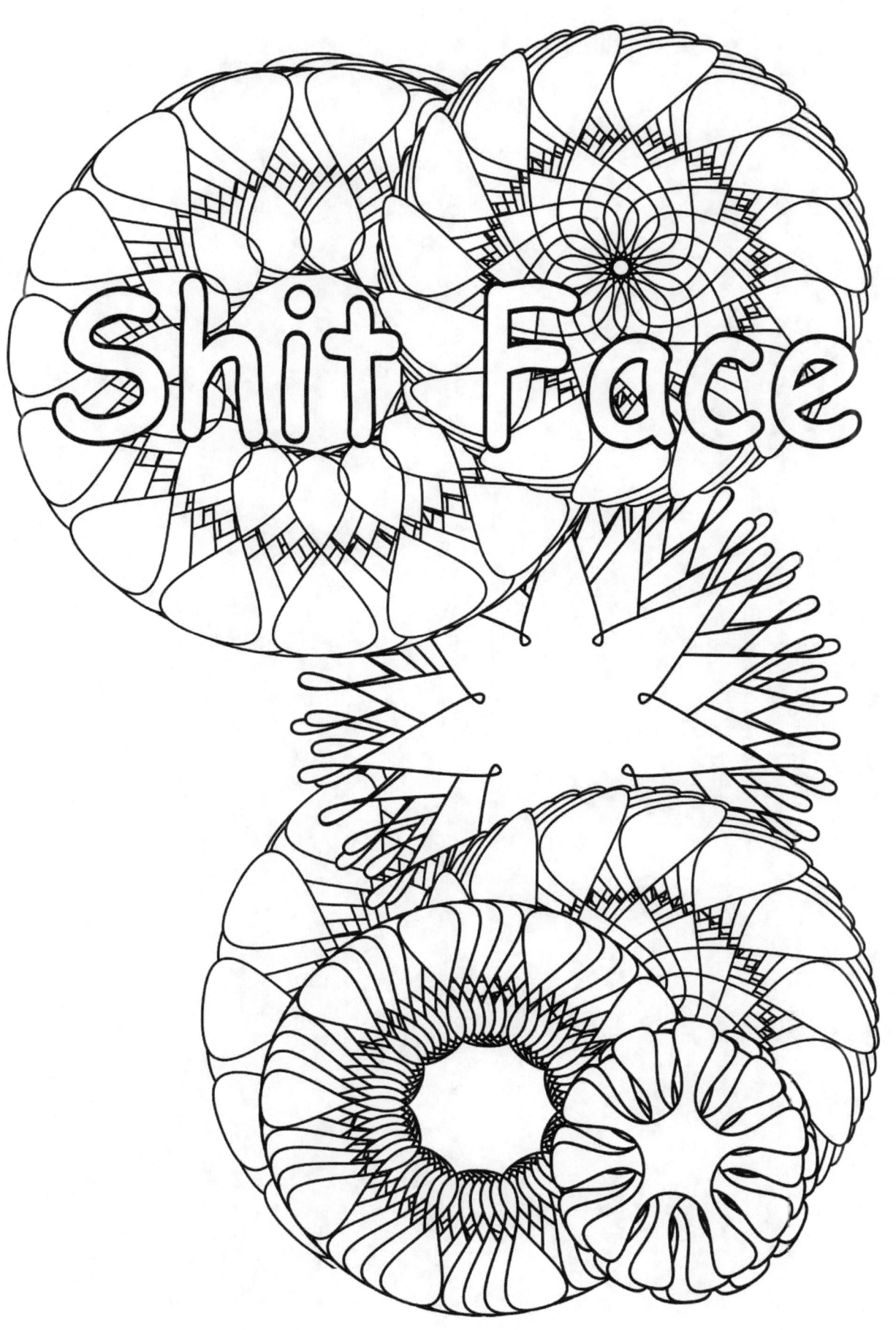

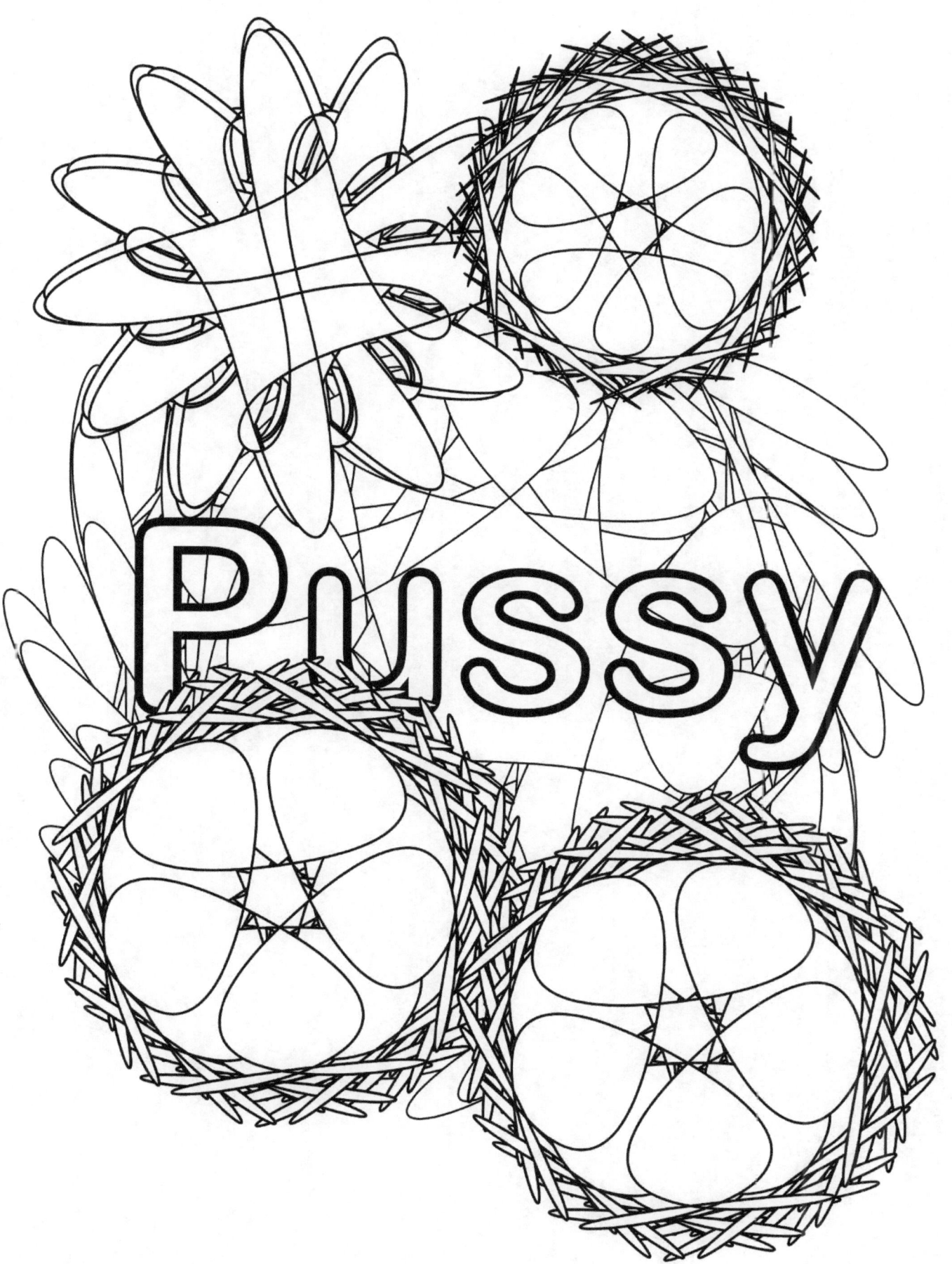

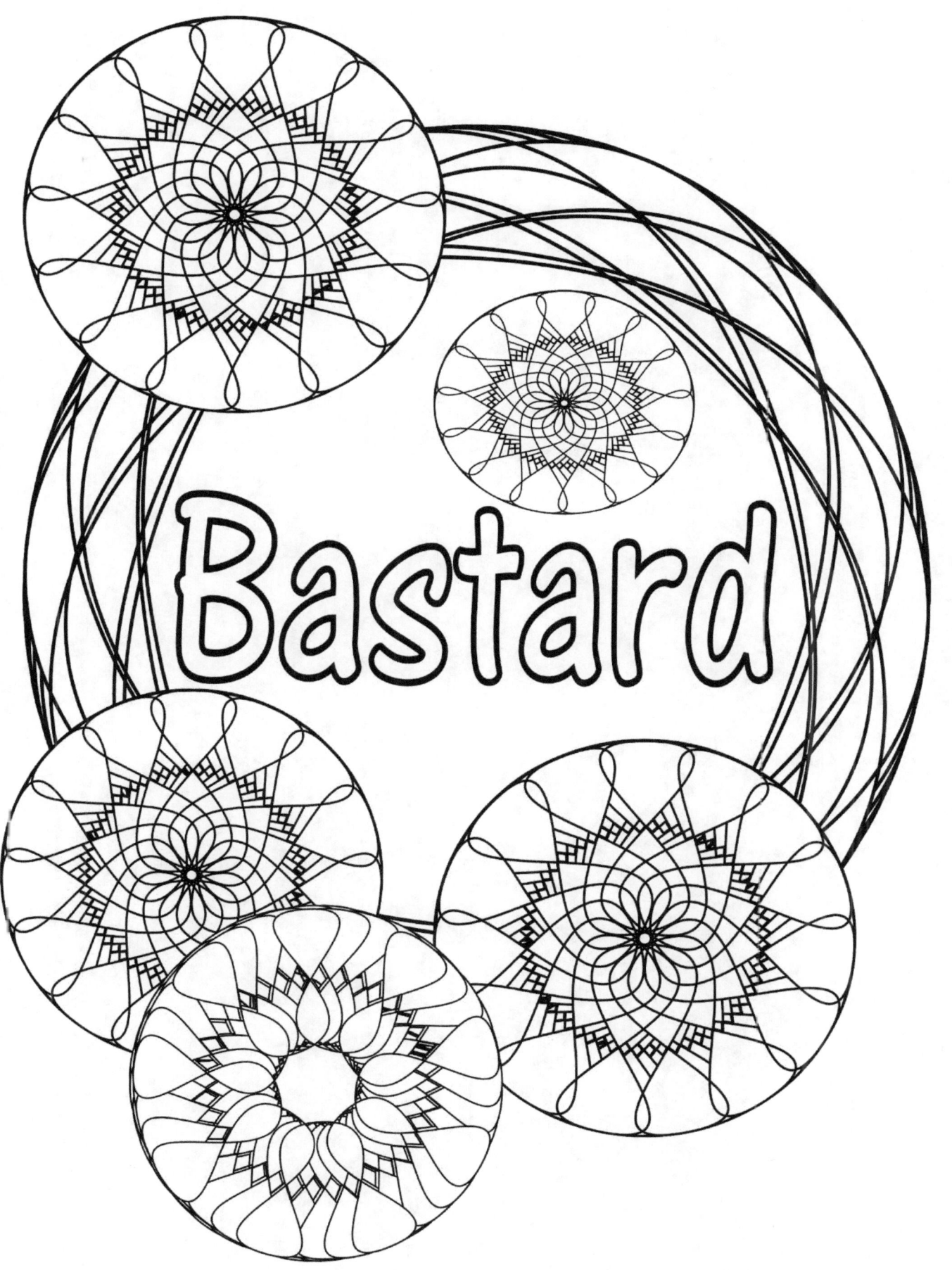

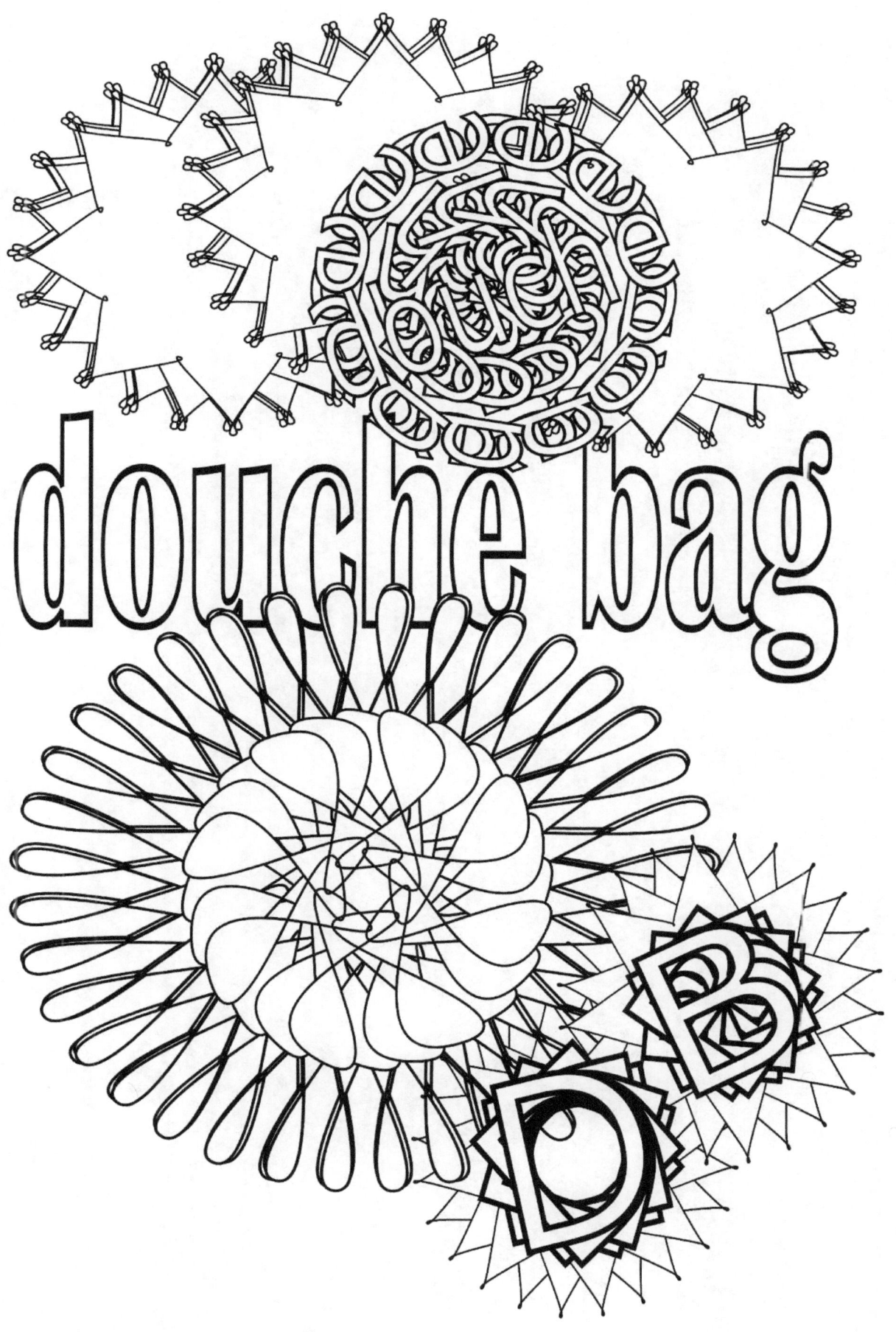

douche bag

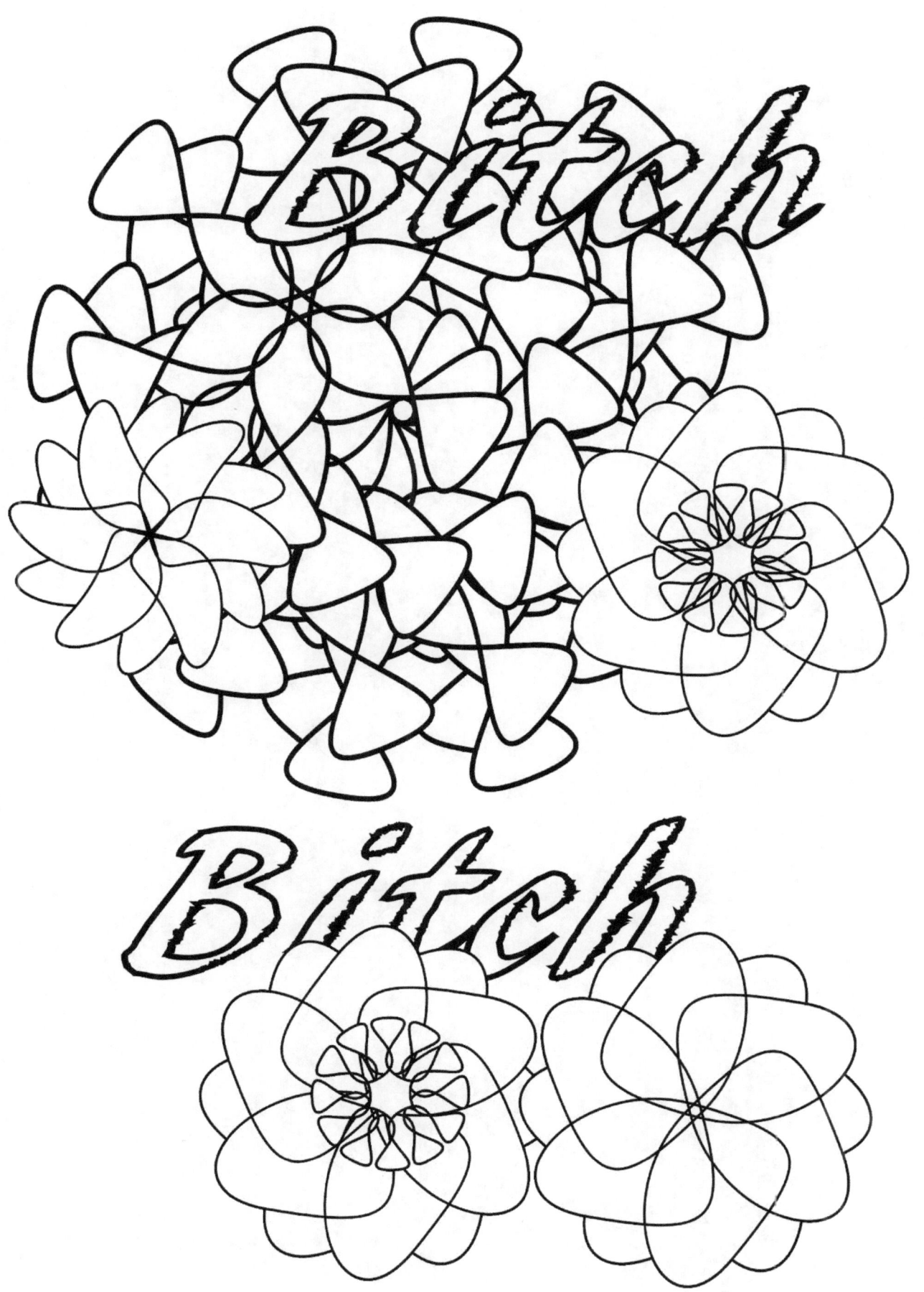

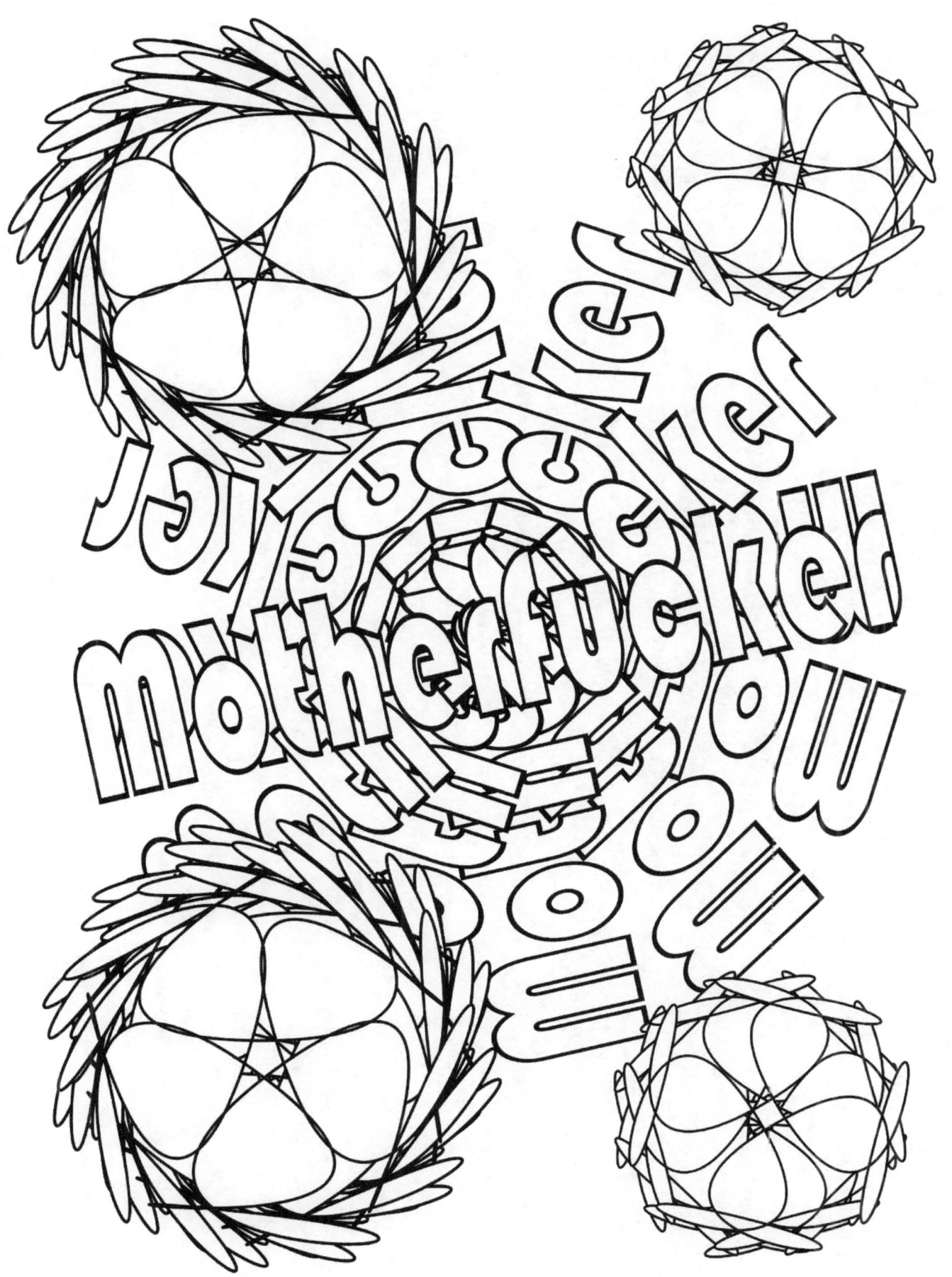

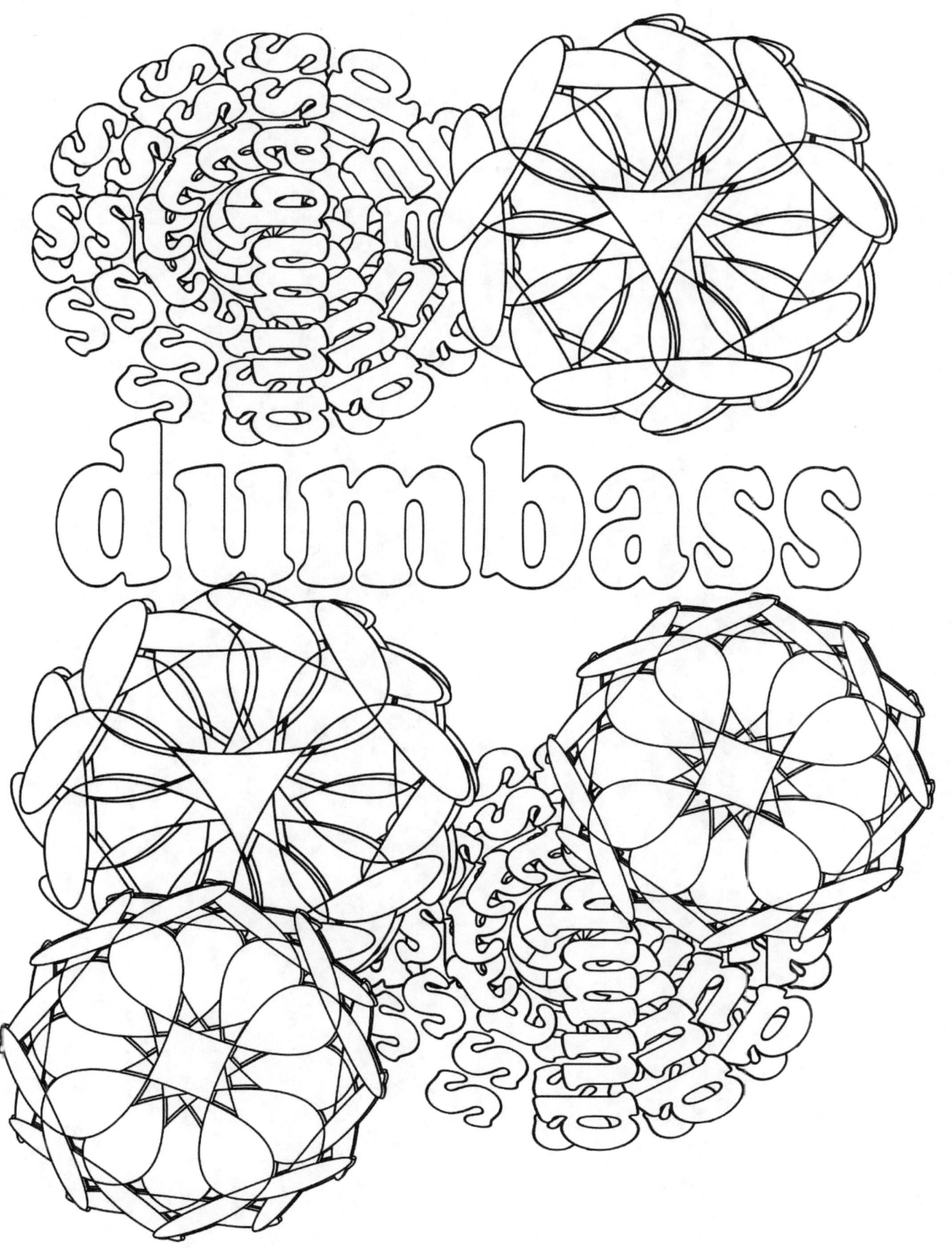

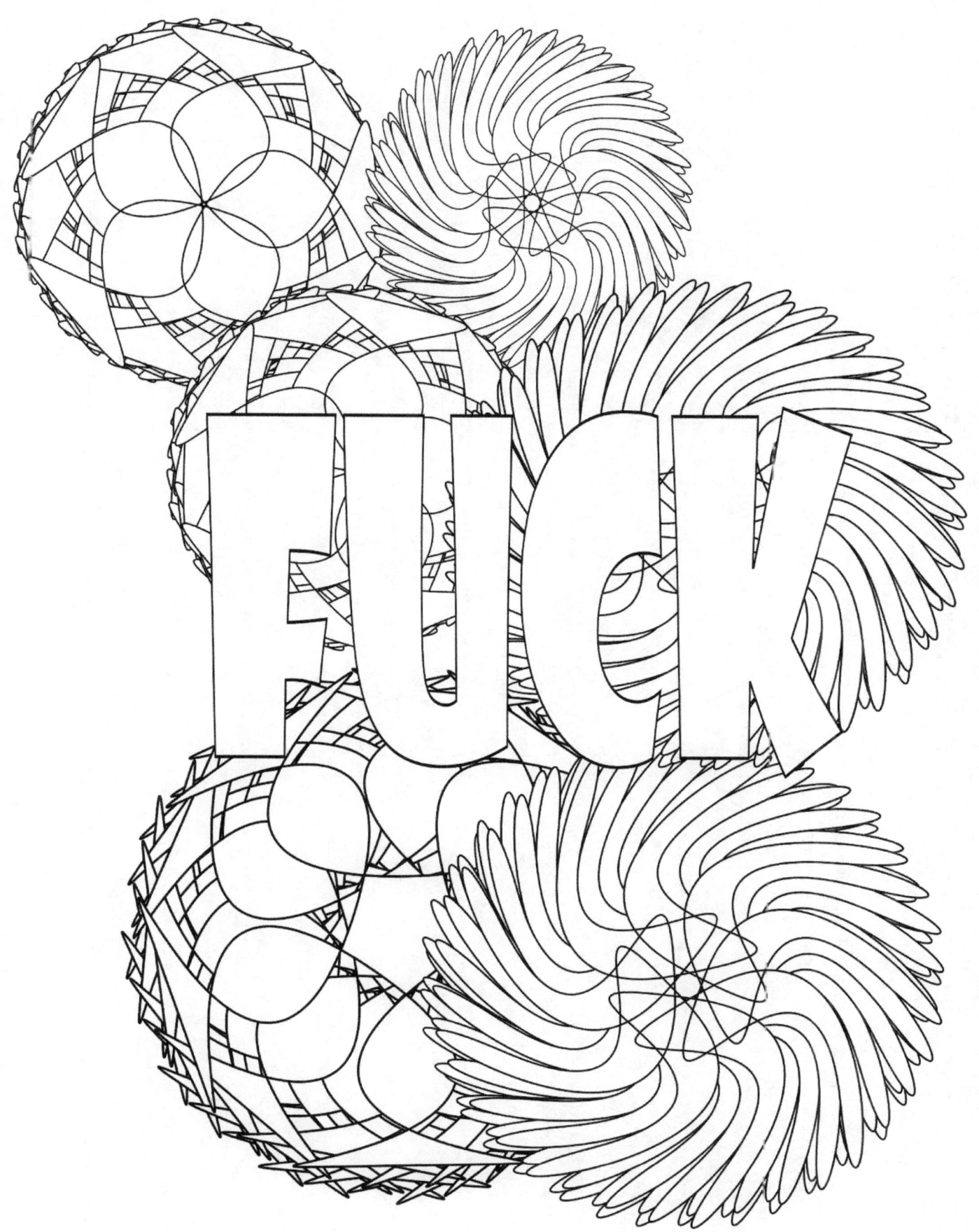

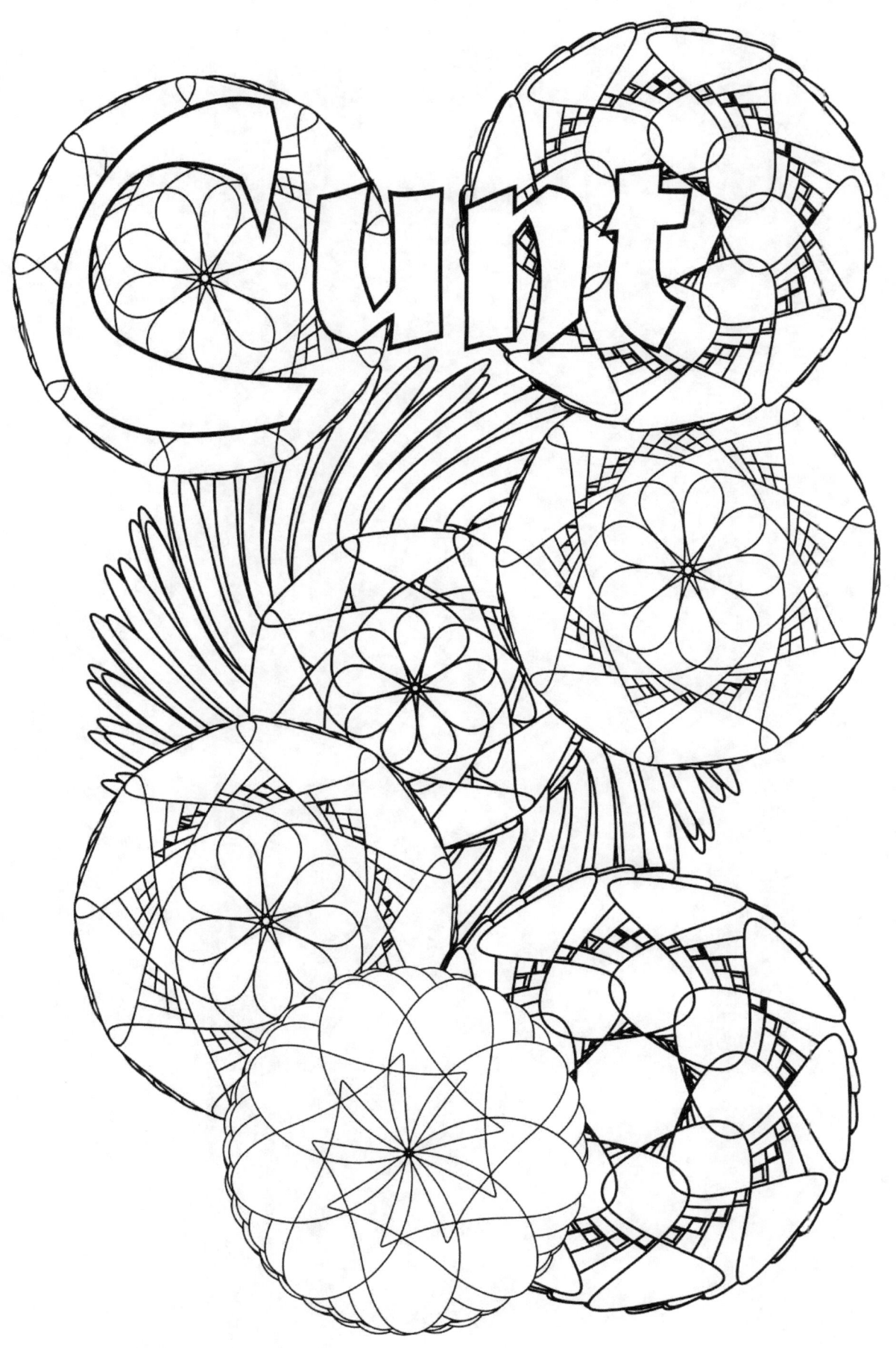

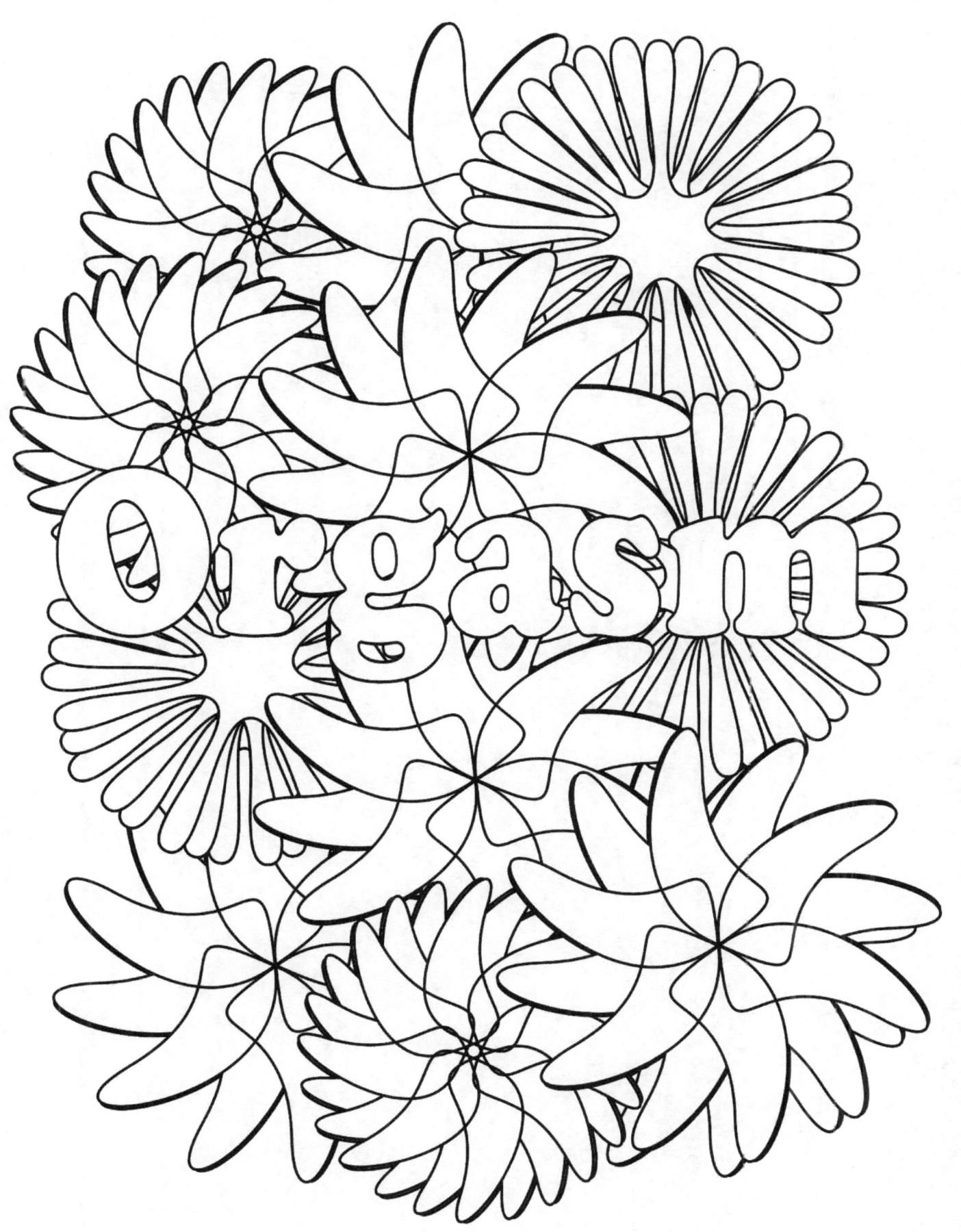

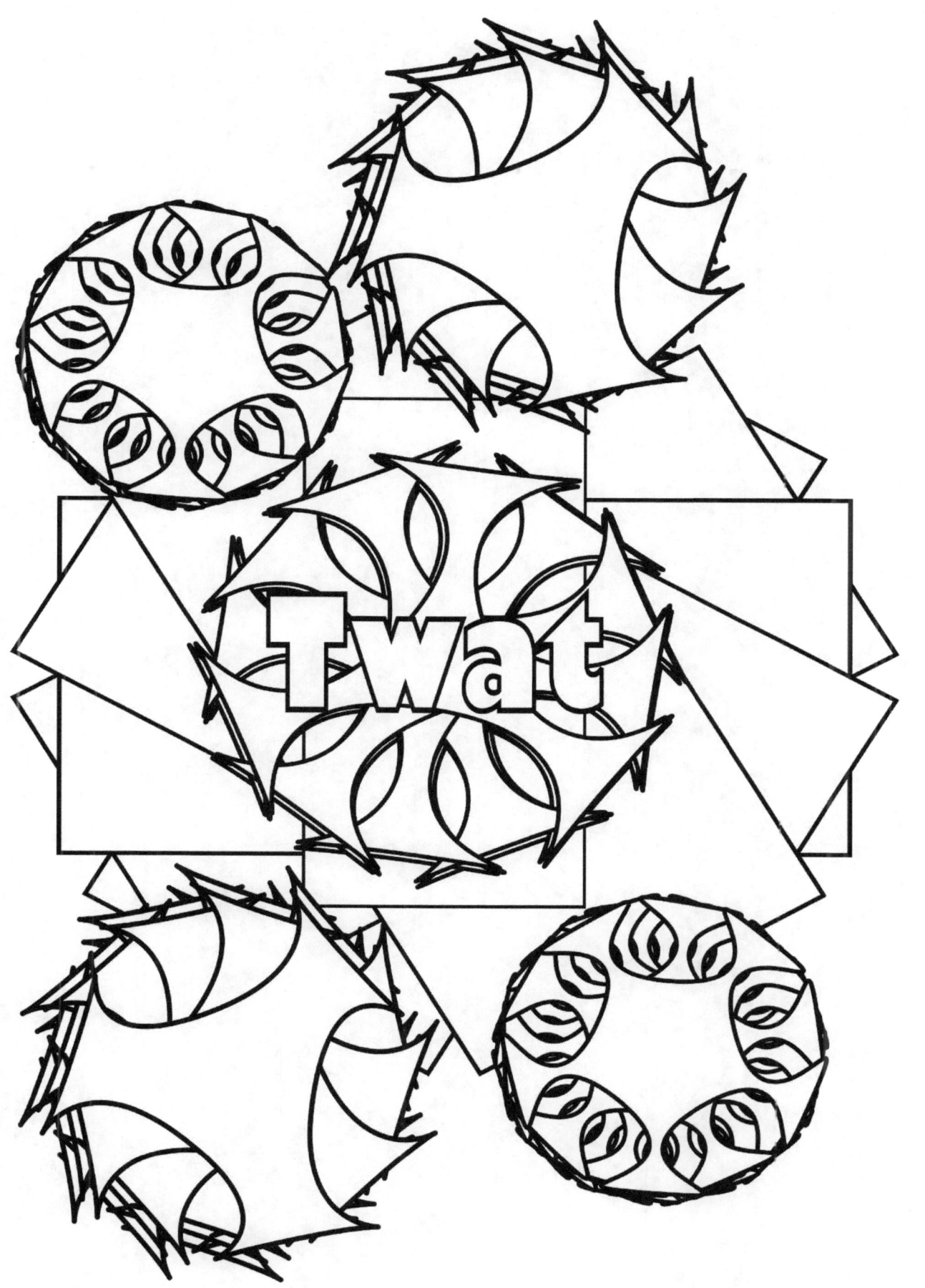

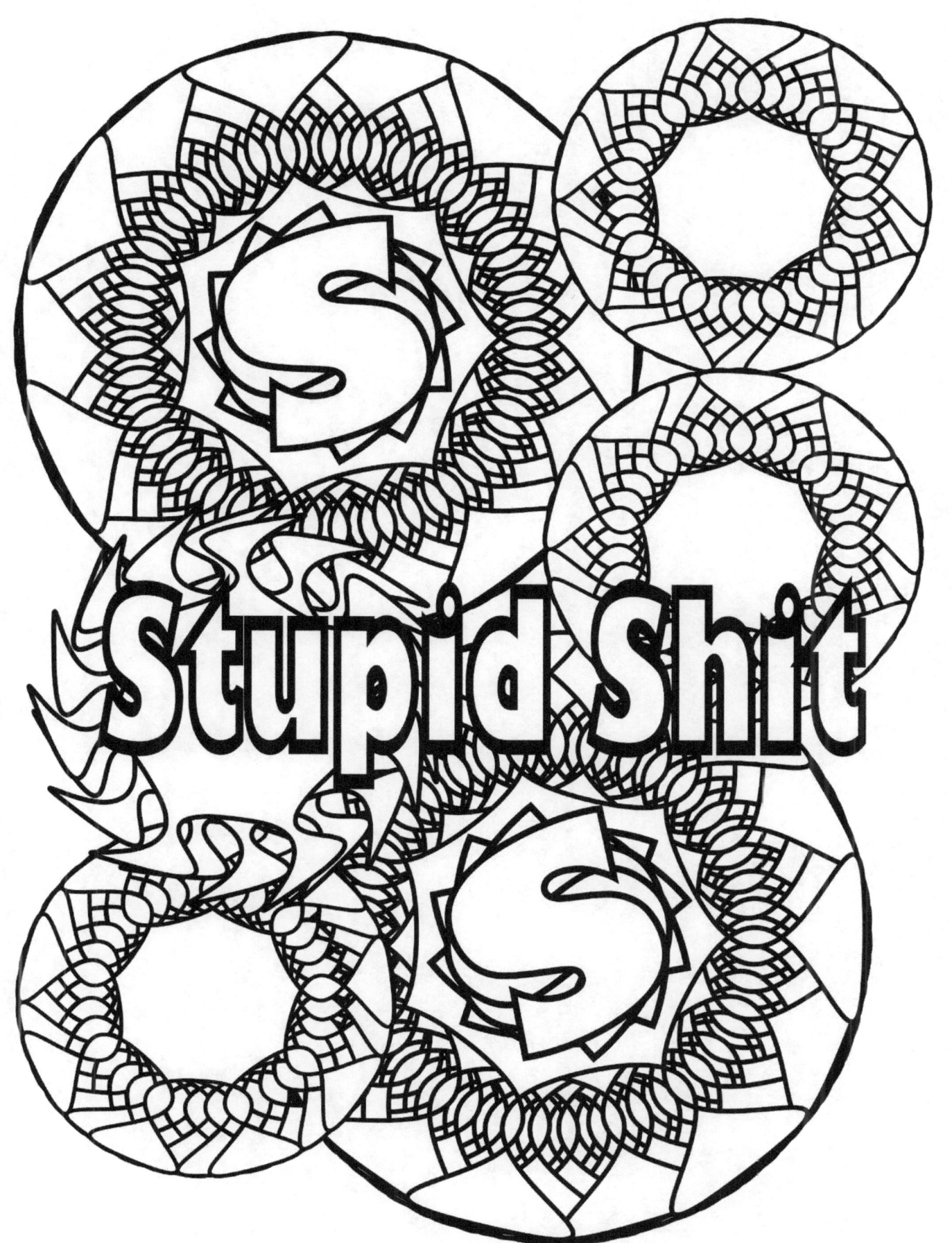

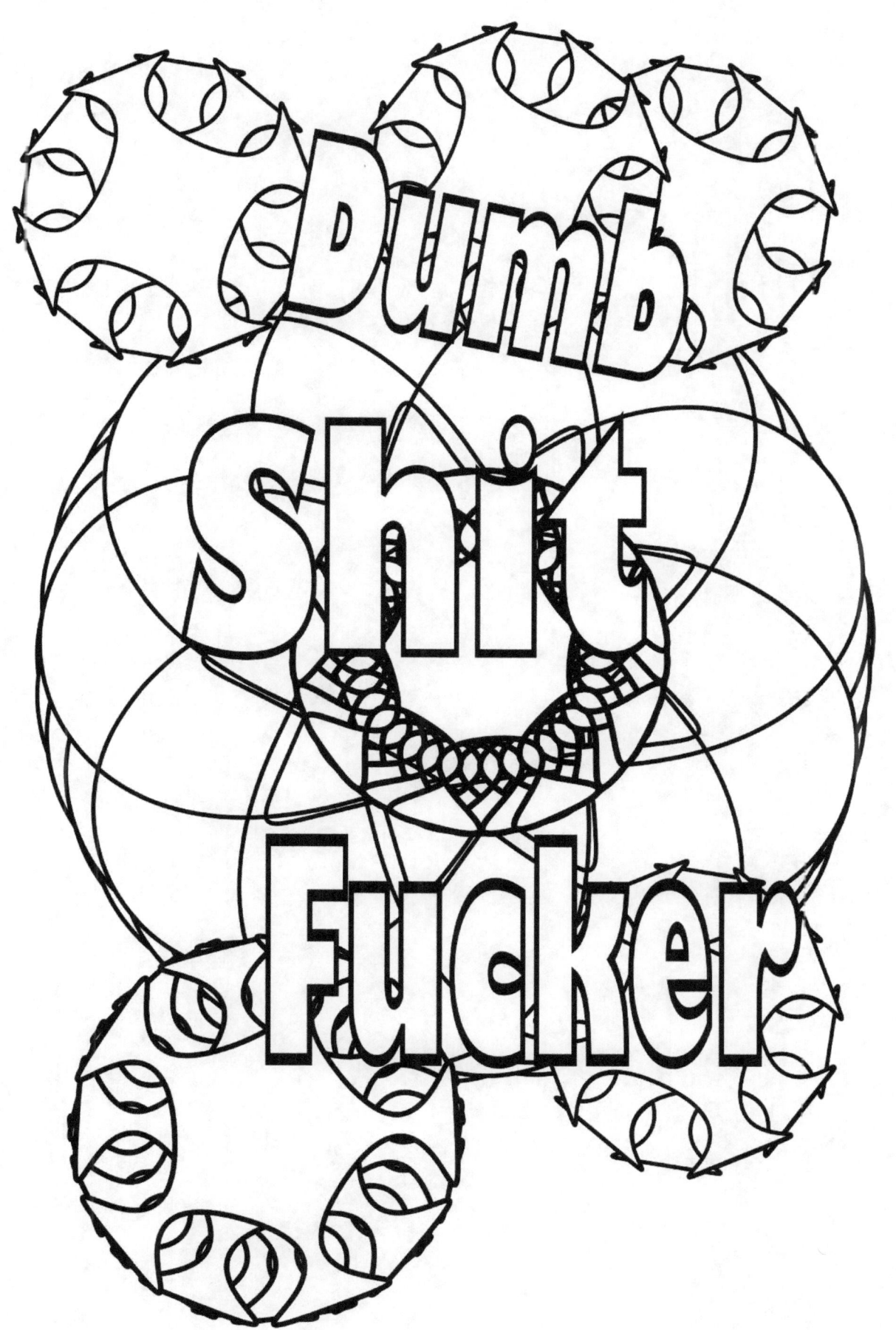

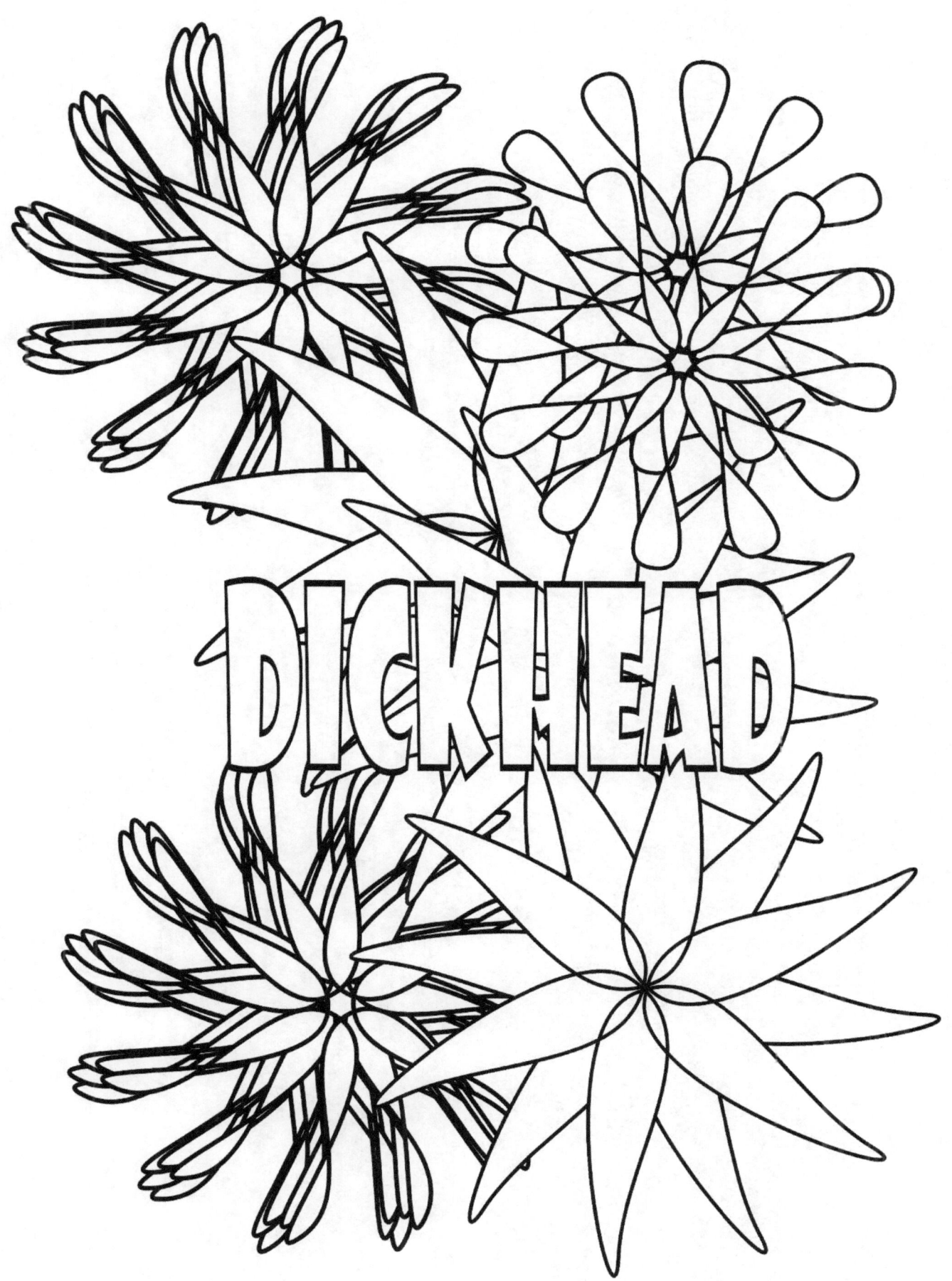

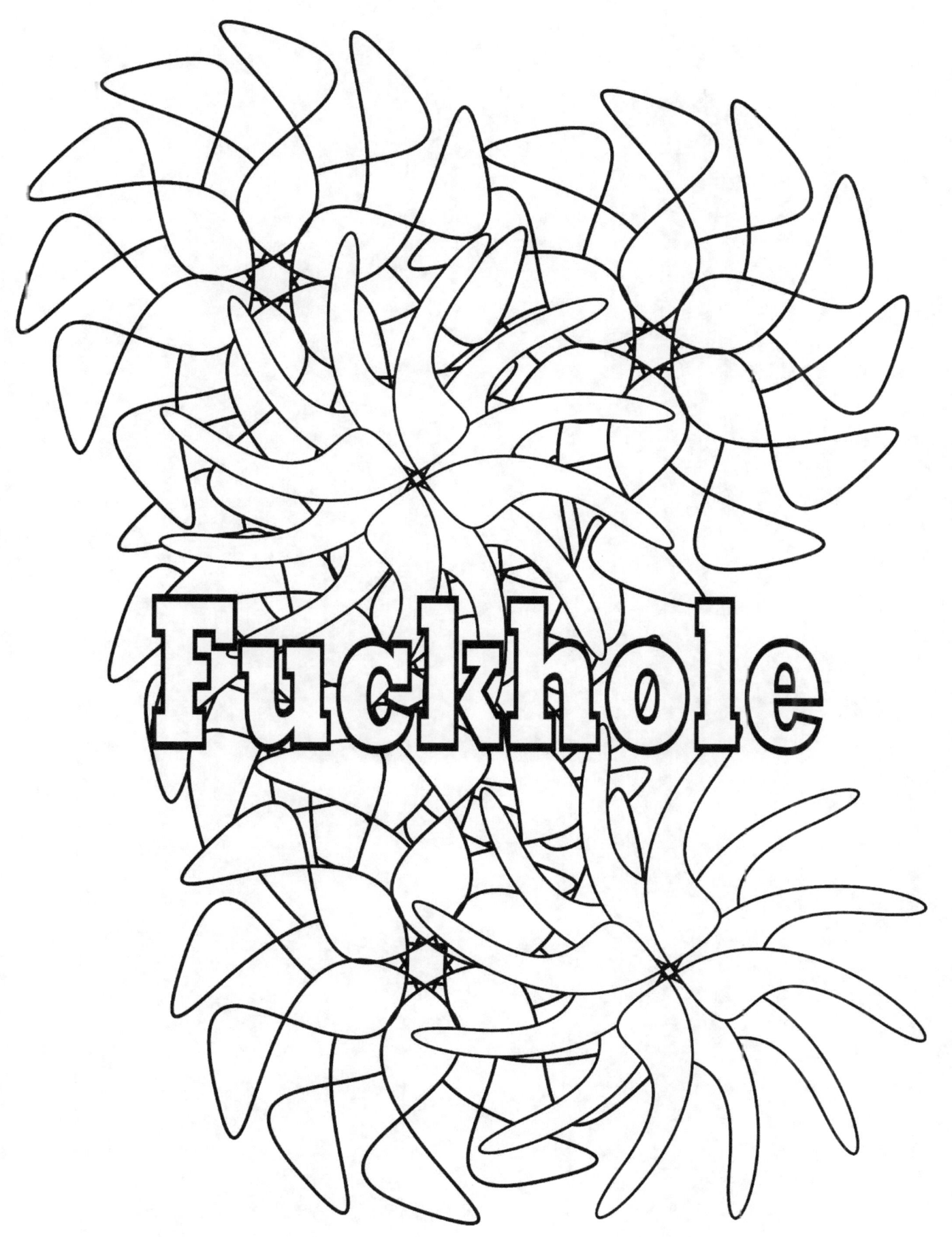

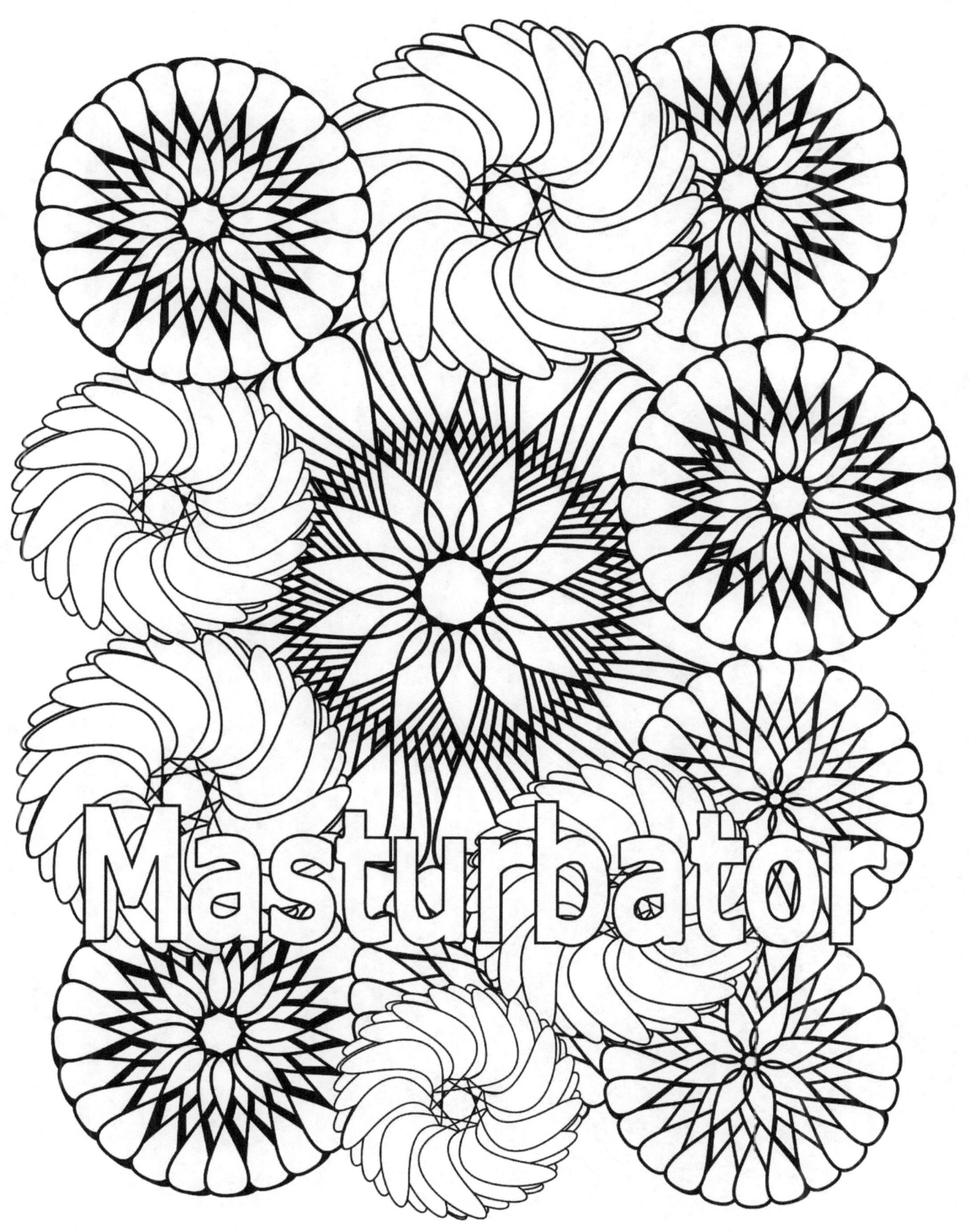

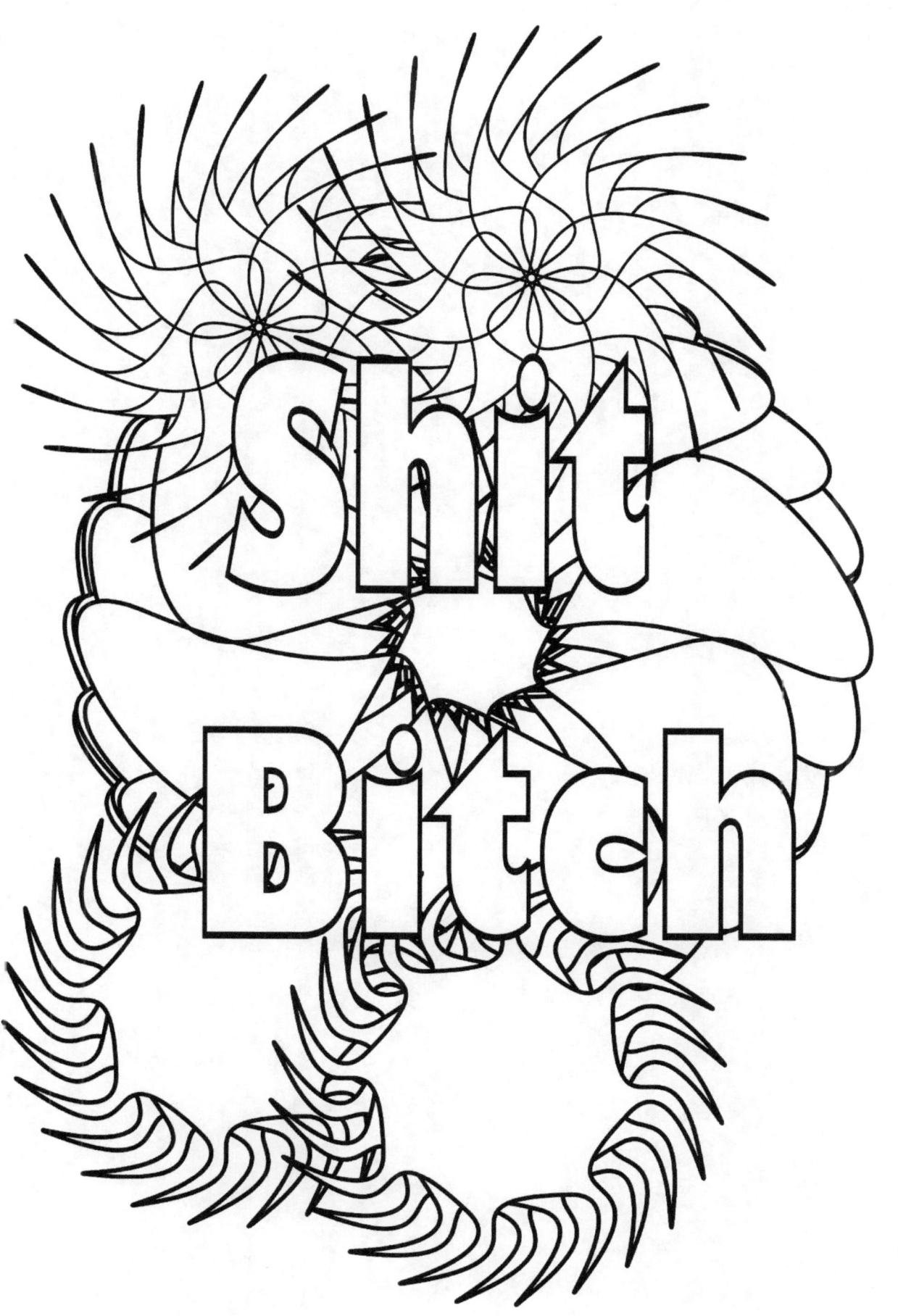

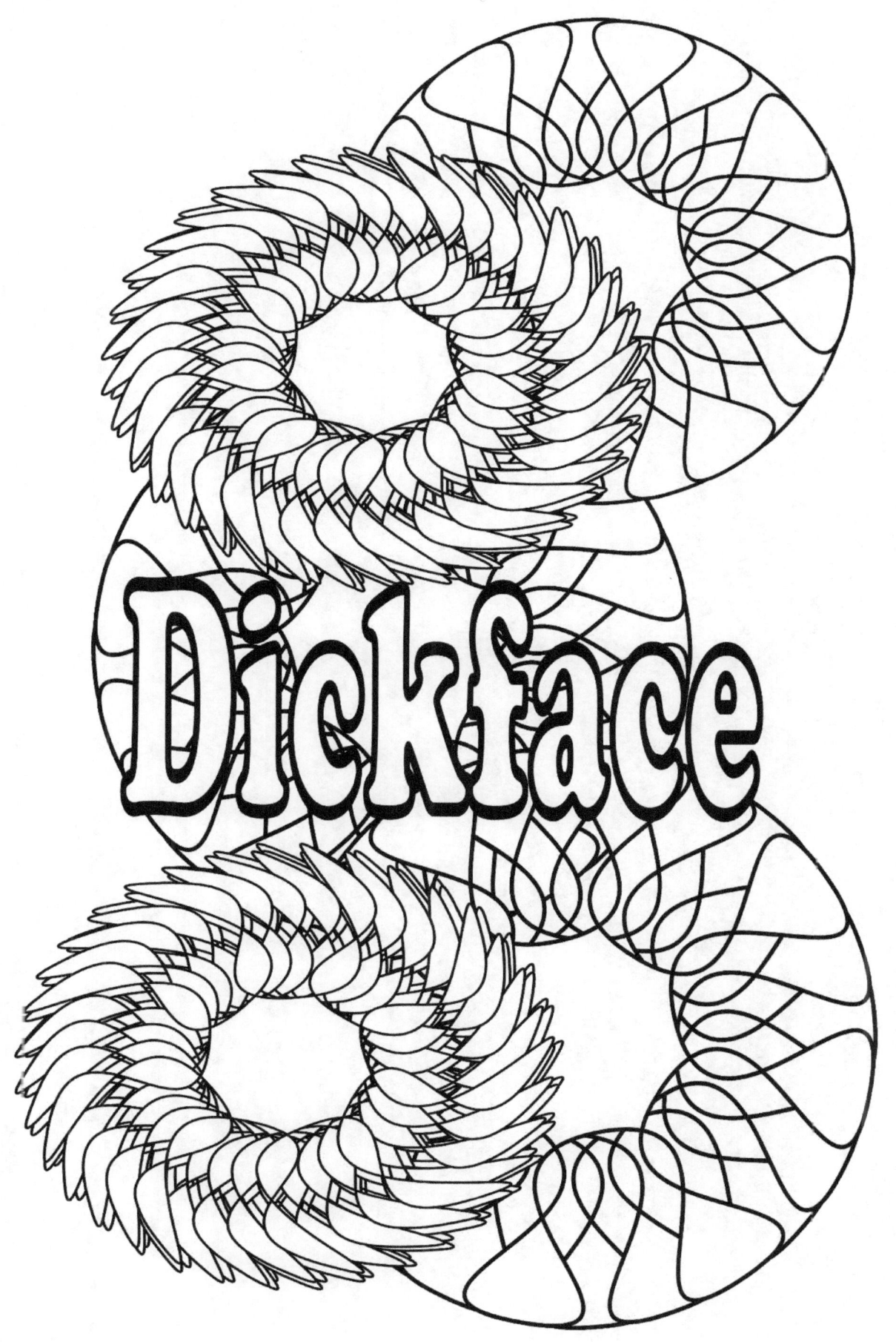

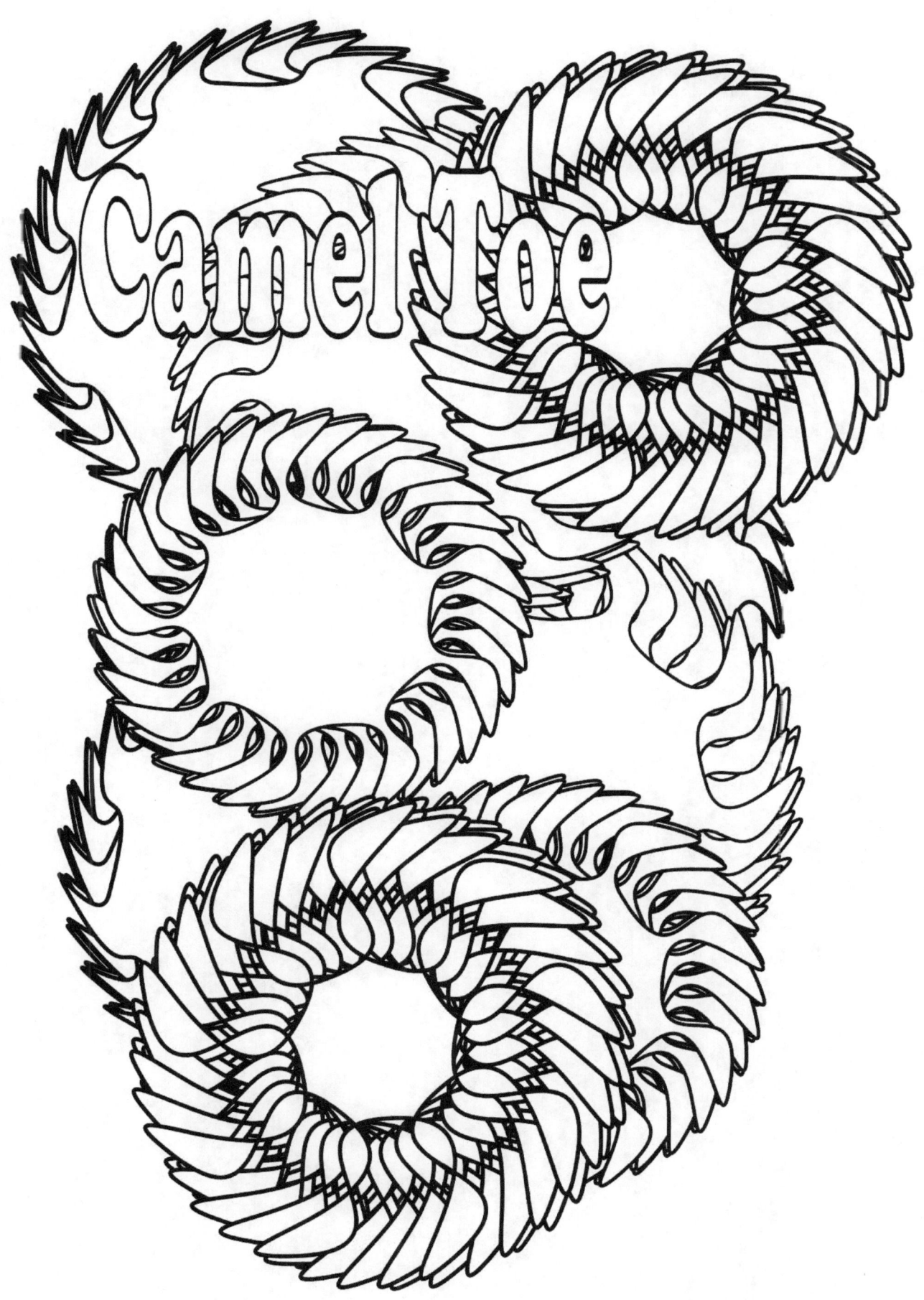

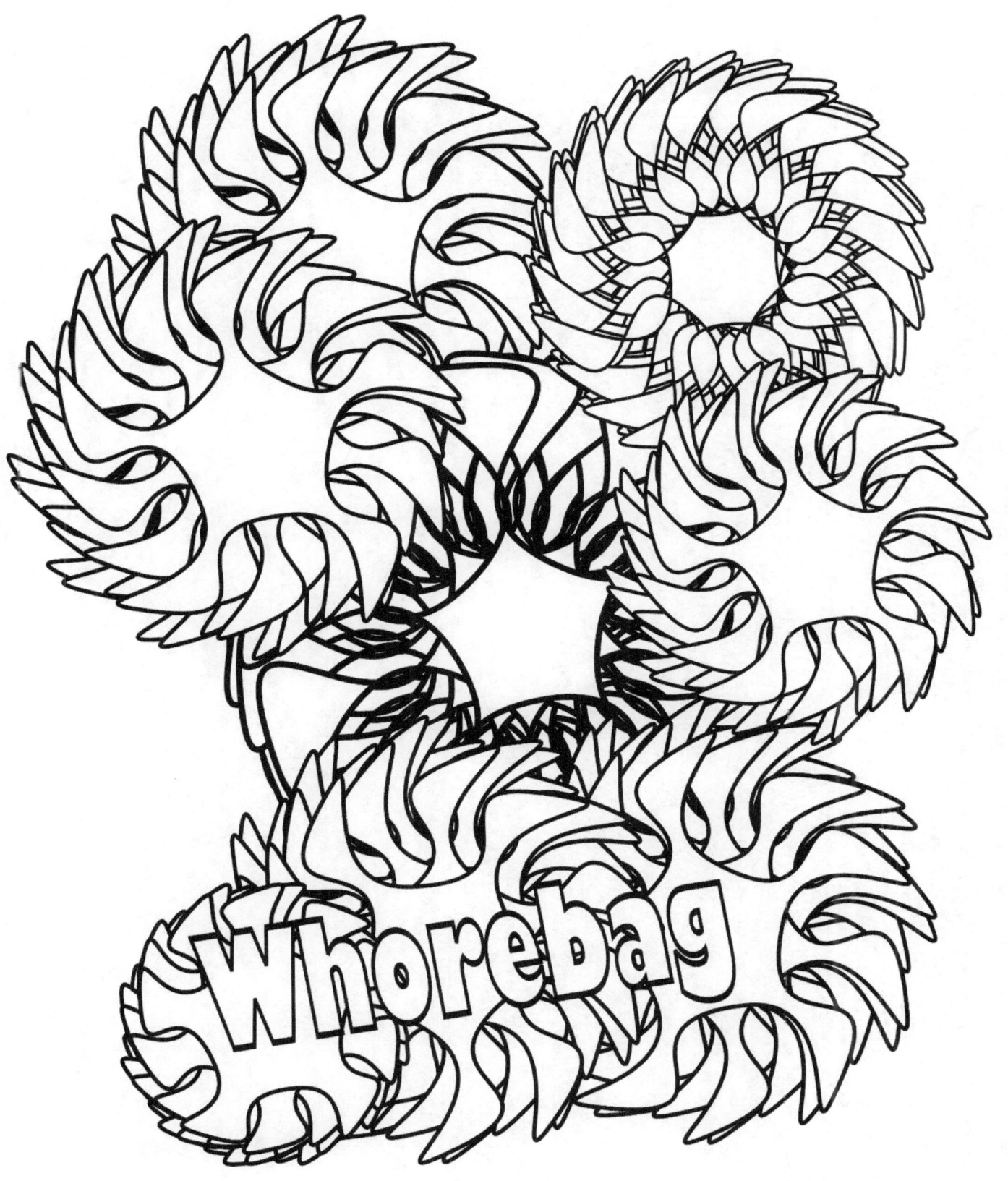

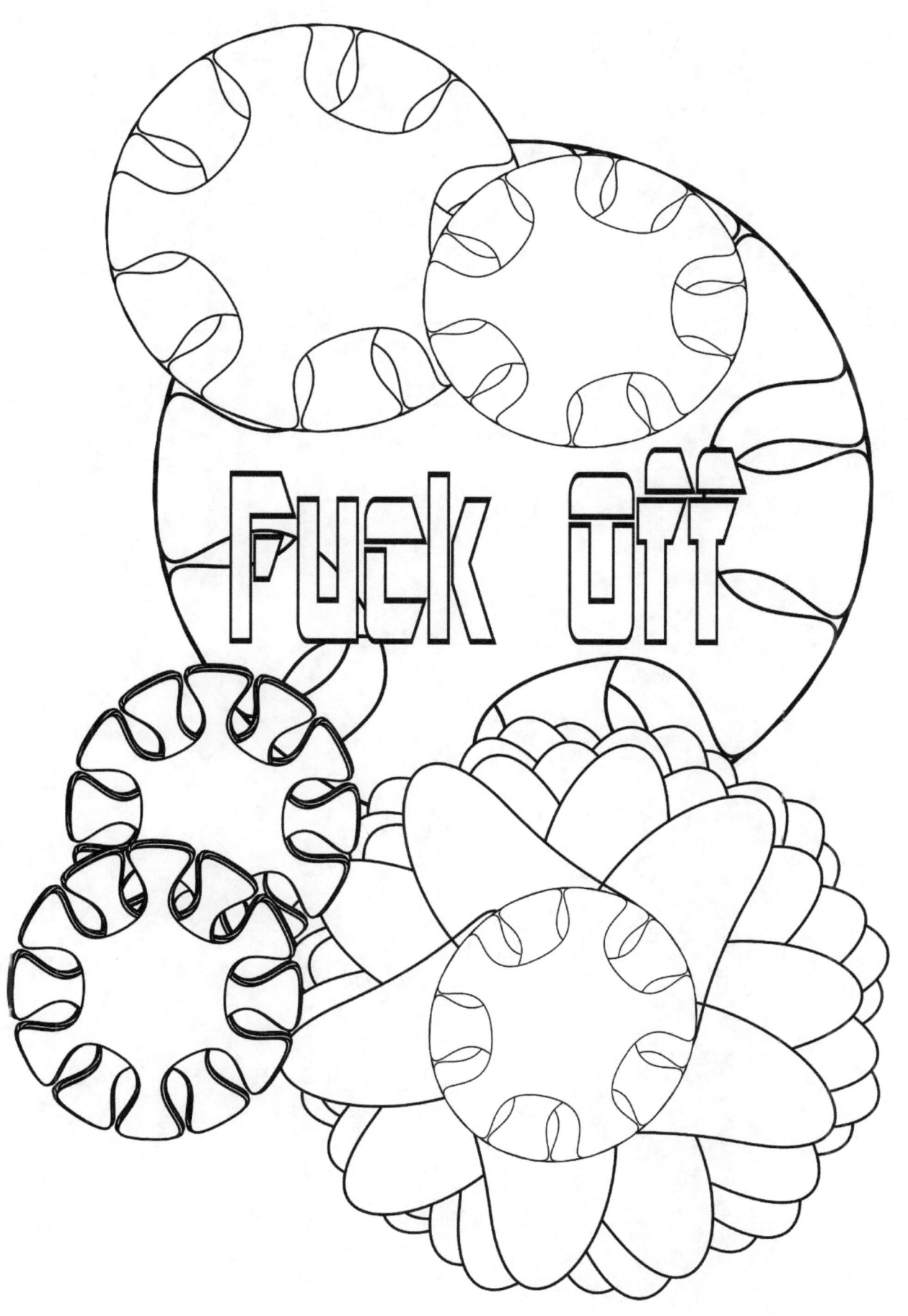

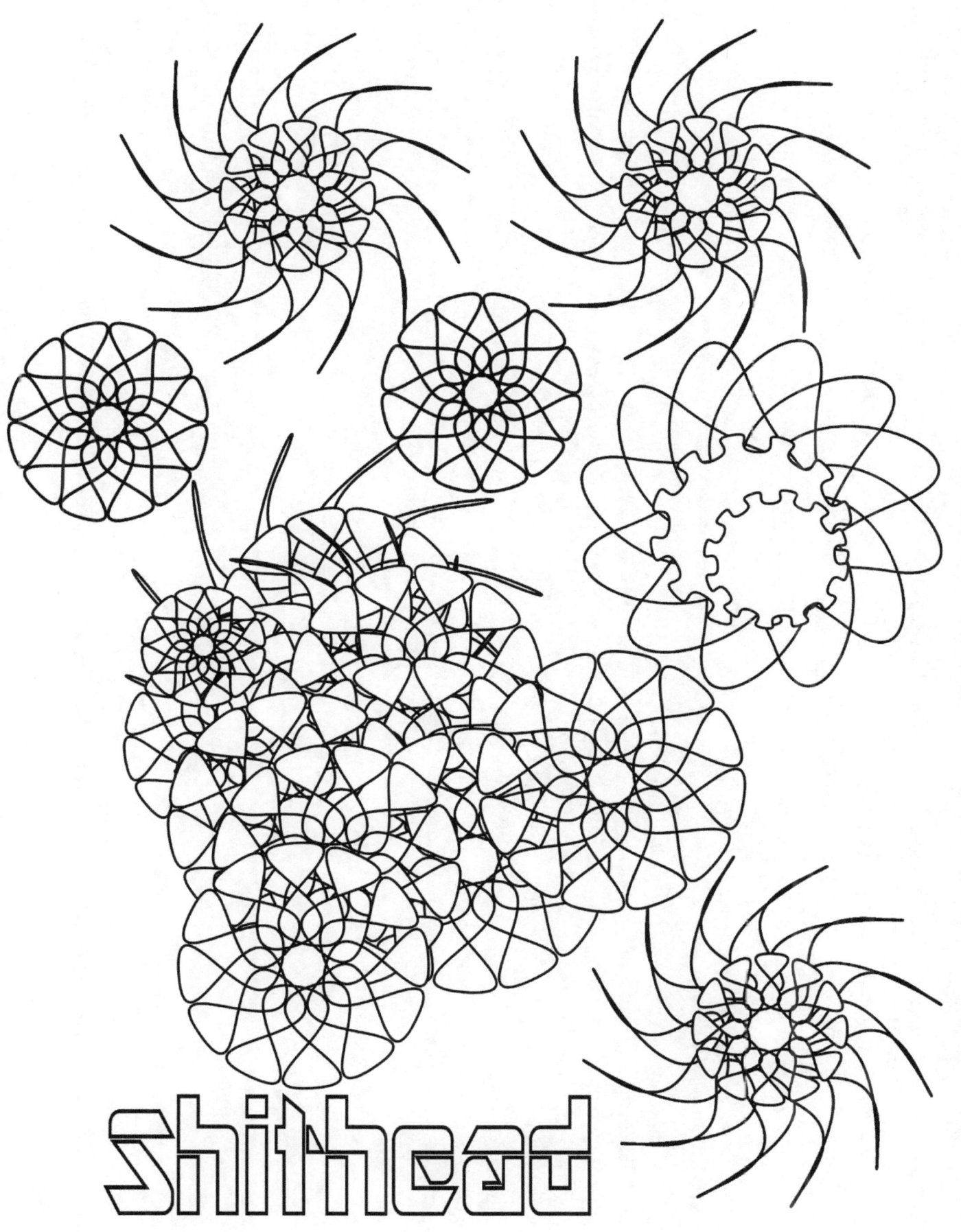

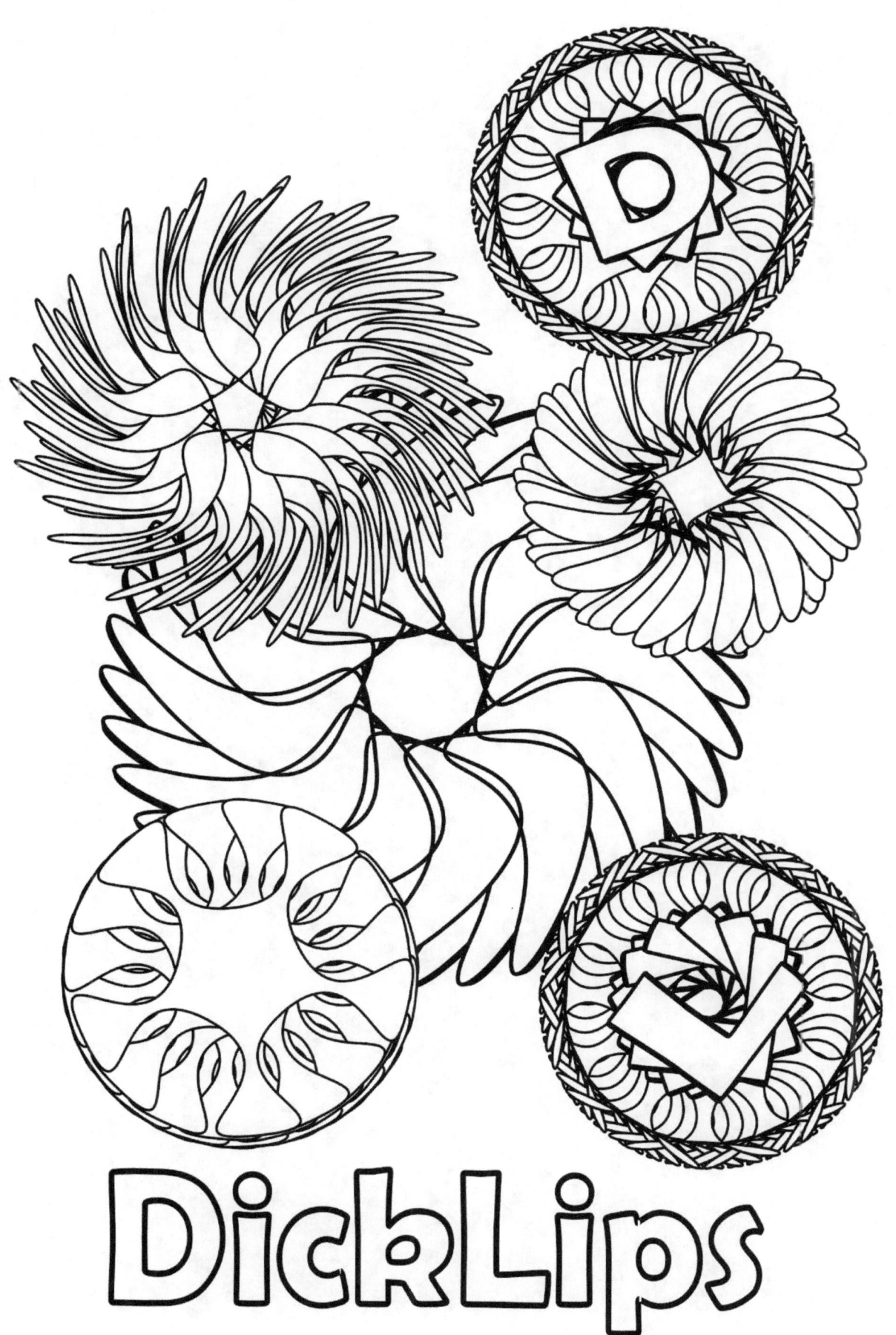

DickLips

www.ingramcontent.com/pod-product-compliance
Lightning Source LLC
Chambersburg PA
CBHW080607190526
45169CB00007B/2914